The Service Pro's Guide to Delighting Diners

50 Tips

TO IMPROVE YOUR

Tips

BY
Bill Marvin
The Restaurant Doctor™

o

HOSPITALITY MASTERS PRESS
PO Box 280 • Gig Harbor, WA 98335

First printing, April 1994
Revision and second printing, March 1995
Third printing, March 1996
Revision and fourth printing, March 1997

ISBN 0-9656262-2-9

ATTENTION ASSOCIATIONS AND MULTI-UNIT OPERATORS:
Quantity discounts are available on this book for premiums, sales
promotions, educational purposes or fund-raising. Custom imprinting or
book excerpts can also be created to meet specific needs.

For more information, please contact our Special Sales Department,
Hospitality Masters Press, PO Box 280, Gig Harbor, WA 98335.
800-767-1055, e-mail: masters@harbornet.com, Fax: 888-767-1055

50 Tips to Improve Your Tips·
CONTENTS

Tips and tipping in the real world
A point to ponder

A POINT TO PONDER:

Service is a mechanical function. It is about serving from the left, clearing from the right and not spilling wine on the tablecloth.

Hospitality, on the other hand, is a human equation. It is a personal gift of caring. It is about me taking care of you . . . because it is YOU, not because you're part of the 75 people who are coming through my station tonight.

You never serve 75 people at a time anyway. You serve one person at a time in 75 different scenarios. It is the quality of those individual interactions — the level of hospitality you provide — that determines your success, both professionally and financially.

- Bill Marvin
  The Restaurant Doctor

Tips and tipping in the real world

You have chosen to make your living, at least for a while, in the hospitality industry — one of the few places people go these days _expecting_ to have a good time. What a great place to be!

A unique feature of the hospitality business is the practice of tipping. For most professional service folks, tips are effectively their entire source of income. Now you can love tipping or you can hate it, but you can't argue that tips are instant feedback on how your guests feel about your work.

The quality of the interaction with your guests not only establishes your income but it also determines how they feel about your restaurant — so in many ways, the success of the business is in your hands!

Every service pro wants to do a better job (and make more money) and this little book can help you do just that. It will give you valuable insights into how you can make your guests feel better-served. It will help you see how to create a relationship with your guests that can cause them to leave you more at the end of the meal and be more anxious to return. If you take these ideas to heart and make them part of your service style, you should see the results where it counts – in your pocket!

There are basically two ways to build your tips – you can increase your sales and/or you can improve the percentage you receive from each sale. Let's look at these two options and how they may figure into your financial future:

Option 1
Increase Your Sales

Tip income is a percentage of what your guests buy, so higher sales are likely to mean greater tips. The approach most people take to build sales is to increase the check through a technique called suggestive selling. Done with sincerity and skill, it can be very effective. Done poorly, it can come across as insincere, shallow and manipulative.

Another problem is that if you focus your attention just on how much money your guests spend, it can be a distraction that can get in the way of establishing personal connection with your guests — and it is personal connection that  determines how well-served your guests feel.

So your tips really come from serving people, not from serving food. If you get the big sale tonight and lose the guests' future business in the process, then pushing the check average was not a very smart strategy for maximizing your income over the long term.

Another way to build sales is to have guests return more often. When you focus on repeat patronage, your goal is to delight your guests rather than simply trying to increase sales (although the two are not necessarily incompatible).

Repeat patronage is the safest way to build sales volume. Take a guest who normally comes in twice a month. If you can treat them in such a way that they come in just one more time a month instead of going to a competitor, you have just increased your sales from this person by 50% – without any increase in the average check and without any pressure on the diner.

Option 2
Increase Your Tip Percentage

If your guests left a bigger percentage of the check as a tip you would also increase your income. So, for example, if your tips went from 10% to 20% of sales, then you could double your income on the same sales volume!

Your tip percentage may be determined in several ways. Some people tip because it is the custom in

this country to tip. (If you have served guests from other countries, you know that in many cultures tipping is definitely <u>not</u> the custom!)

Some people will leave a tip, even if the service was poor, because they would feel guilty if they didn't.

But the biggest factor in tipping — the thing that will determine whether diners leave you 10% or 30% — is the level of personal connection you can establish with your guests.

The greater the bond that is created, the higher your tip is likely to be. At the least, when the guest is deciding what to leave you at the end of the meal, personal connection will cause them to round <u>up</u> a dollar instead of rounding down!

Do you have regulars who always ask for you? Do you typically get a better tip from them than you do from the run-of-the-mill public? Have you ever taken home more total tips from a four-table station than a six-table station? If so, it shows you what personal connection can do for your financial well-being!

The good news is that the same thing can happen with virtually every table . . . and it can happen more often than not!

Is this idea interesting? Read on and you will start to understand how it is done!

1

Be competent

Exceptional "people skills" can certainly help improve your tips but human relations ability alone won't be enough to save you if you can't handle the basic elements of your job well.

You must know your menu, be able to match the pace of service to the needs of the guests, handle the check properly and learn to juggle a hundred other details. Once you have mastered the technical parts of the job, it will be easier to keep a clear head and focus on the human dimensions of your work.

Memorable service is almost invisible to your guests because it doesn't draw their attention away from the meal experience. Inept service is like fingernails on the blackboard and can destroy the dining event. Be a pro. Get the details of your job down cold.

2

Get a good night's rest

I know, you are young and it's almost your duty to work all day and party all night! Don't get me wrong — I'm all for having a good time but it is hard to stay sharp and focused when you are running on three hours sleep. Just being awake and functioning does not necessarily mean you are able to deliver top notch service.

Fatigue causes you to become distracted more easily . . . and distractions interfere with your ability to connect with your guests. Remember personal connection determines how well-served your guests feel . . . and whether they will leave you 10% or 30%!

The simple message here is that proper rest is like money in your pocket. Do your guests (and your bank account) a favor and get your sleep!

3

Get into character before you step onstage

People go out to restaurants for a good time as well as a good meal. This makes food-service an entertainment experience and you are the Master of Ceremonies!

Getting into character means you take a shower *every day* before coming to work, your hair and nails are clean, your breath is fresh and you're wearing a clean uniform that fits. When you look the part, you act the part.

Getting into character also means putting personal issues on hold until your shift is over. We all have problems at home but you can't do anything about them while you are at work. Cluttering your head with personal issues on the job will only make it harder to connect with your guests and cost you money. Give yourself a break!

4

Be sure the tabletop is picture-perfect

A positive first impression helps put your guests in a better frame of mind and gives them reasons to expect that their meal experience is going to be special. A few extra seconds will help assure that you won't lose points before the meal even gets started.

Smooth out the table cloth, straighten the condiments, align the silver. Be sure the glassware is sparklingly spotless and the silverware is clean. Square up the chairs with the place settings. Be sure salt and pepper shakers aren't greasy, the flowers are fresh and the ashtrays are clean and dry.

If you know your guests are celebrating a special occasion, why not decorate the table? It can be a nice surprise that might just gain you a few points!

5

Offer a sincere compliment

People love to be complimented — don't you? They also can tell the difference between honest praise and deceitful flattery.

It is a nice touch to notice something personal and positive about your guests. If a man has on a great tie or if a woman is wearing an interesting pin — and if it seems appropriate — offering a sincere compliment can help create a more personal relationship with the guest and do you both a lot of good!

The key ideas are <u>appropriate</u> and <u>sincere</u> — empty words won't work. You see, the real message is always carried in the feeling behind the words you use, not by the words themselves. People can sense a con. If what you say is not honest, you can lose the guest's trust and therefore their business.

6

Acknowledge guests within 60 seconds

Were you ever seated in a restaurant only to wait . . . and wait? Do you recall how that affected your mood? Would it surprise you to learn that there is a relationship between a person's mood and their enjoyment of the meal? Would you expect a better tip from a guest in a good mood or a bad one?

Your initial contact sets the tone for the rest of the meal. Guests just feel more comfortable if they know the server is aware that they are waiting. The longer they sit without contact, the more irritated they get.

Even if you are busy, come to the table, stop, focus your attention, smile, extend a friendly welcome and let them know you will be right back. If you are too buried to start their service within three minutes, ask for help.

7

Engage your brain before operating your mouth

How does it feel when you talk to someone who is not listening to you or whose mind is wandering while they speak? Pretty annoying, right? Your guests feel the same displeasure whenever *you* operate on "automatic."

When you address guests while your mind is distracted, your clear message is that something is more important to you than they are. This will not help them feel well served or think of you kindly when it is time to figure the tip!

Approach the table, STOP and clear your head of stray thoughts. Wait for your guests to look up at you. When they do, be clear about what you have to say . . . and say it with a smile in your voice.

8

Look at guests when you speak to them

You won't make points by talking to the table cloth or your order pad. When speaking to a guest, clear your head, try to engage their eyes and smile. Even if they do not look back at you, they will sense your focus.

When addressing a table of guests, shift your attention from one diner to another every five seconds or so and speak <u>only</u> to the person whom you are looking at. You will hold the attention of the entire table and they will *all* feel better served.

Another thing: never talk to a table while you are moving. When you do, you are effectively saying you have something more important to do and you do not want to be delayed. The result is that you look like a jerk and your guests feel less significant.

9

Learn and use guests' names

Nothing sounds better to people than the respectful use of their own names. It is a degree of caring that clearly shows guests how important they are to you.

How can you get their names? Ask the greeter to drop you a card with the guest's name off the reservation list. Ask a veteran co-worker for the name of a familiar-looking diner. Convention guests often leave their name tags on! When all else fails, ask them!

However you do it, greet guests by name when you first get to the table and use the name as appropriate during the meal. Don't address guests by their first names unless they ask you to. Repeated use of names will help you learn who your guests are and your tips will reflect your additional effort.

10

Remember what guests like and don't like

At the most basic level, this means remembering what the guests tell you during this meal. Does she want water without ice? Is he drinking decaf? If so, they shouldn't have to tell you twice.

As you become more adept as service, you will start to remember what your diners preferred the last time they came in and automatically accommodate those desires on their future visits without a reminder.

It is a great way to make guests feel welcome. It is also a big part of the reason why most servers say they get a better tip from the regular guests who ask to be seated at their station. Is it starting to sound like a good idea to keep a few notes on what your regular guests like? It should.

11

Keep your mind off the tip

A healthy tip results from taking proper care of your guests and creating a personal connection with them. Interestingly, when you fixate on the reward (the tip), it is a distraction that can prevent you from giving your full attention to the activities and attitudes that will actually cause the guest to want to leave you that reward.

When you are distracted, your guests are more likely to feel unserved and less inclined to leave a good tip. Strange as it seems at first, if you don't think about your tip at all during the meal, you are likely to earn more.

So what do you think about? Nothing! Keep your head clear and deal only with what is happening at the moment. Time will fly, you will stay out of the weeds and your guests will have a better time!

12

Observe common courtesies

It is unfortunate that common courtesy is not very common anymore. However, its general lack of use does create opportunities to pick up points with your guests.

Address guests as "Mr." or "Ms." and use terms like "Sir" or "Ma'am." Always say "Thank you" and "You're welcome." These are simple courtesies but they can sound like music to your guests' ears after years of "Yo, dude, what it is?" and the disrespectful way people typically seem to relate to each other elsewhere in our society.

After all, foodservice is the hospitality business and the gift of hospitality is our most important product. Treating guests with respect is a very hospitable (and very profitable) thing to do!

13

Focus on delighting your guests

It is very easy to define service from the perspective of the provider. ("Did you give them good service?" "Yes, I did.") But good service from the server's viewpoint might not necessarily be as good from the guests' side of the table.

However, if your goal to <u>delight</u> your guests, it will force you to look at the entire dining experience from the guest's perspective... and that is the only one that counts anyway!

Many of the ideas in this little book can delight your guests but they are only a hint of what might be possible. If you can keep a clear head, you will be more sensitive to what your guests want. Give your guests a few pleasant surprises during the meal and just watch how your income will grow!

14

Make personal recommendations

Guests don't come to the restaurant to be students of your menu. In fact, figuring out many restaurant menus can be a career in itself! Offering a personal recommendation is a special gift for your guests.

Turn them onto something good. Tell them what <u>you</u> like. Let them in on a secret. Tell them what <u>you</u> think is the best thing on the menu. Don't try to guess what they want. You can't do it. It is OK to have an opinion. If they want something else, they will ask.

Be sure you have tasted everything on the menu so that you can speak from your personal experience instead of from a memorized script. Remember that it is your enthusiasm and sincerity that will make the recommendation personal.

15

Introduce yourself last

The server introduction ("Hi, my name is _____ and I'll be your waiter tonight") is both stale and boring. Many servers just do it without thinking . . . but you know the risk of speaking without thinking.

The sad truth is that when you first approach the table, guests don't know you well enough to <u>care</u> who you are! Wait until you have finished your initial contact at the table and then offer your name if you feel comfortable doing it. ("By the way, my name is Karen. If you need anything, just stand on your chair, yell HELP and I'll be right over!")

The good news is that it is much harder to stiff "Karen" than it is to stiff "the server." Since creating a more personal connection generally leads to bigger tips, you are on your way!

16

Suggest alternatives to sold-out items

If you are doing things right, you will not always have everything that is listed on your menu. While you may not have control of what is available, you *always* have control of the way you handle the situation.

If you are out of stock on an item, immediately suggest another item you think will work. If you just announce that you are out and say nothing more, you will leave the guests wondering what to do next. They will feel less comfortable and that will have a negative effect on their meal experience.

Remember that you always <u>sell</u> out, you never <u>run</u> out! The distinction is subtle but when you consider the impact on your guests, you will understand why the distinction is important.

17

Offer reading material to single diners

Job One is to make sure the guests have a good time. Single diners can be a particular challenge because they do not have the companionship and conversation of their table mates to help pass the time.

Make it easy on them. Leave the menu on the table a little longer. Ask if they have seen today's paper and bring one if they want it. If they have brought "homework" with them (usually a book or briefcase), seat them at a table with good lighting. If it seems appropriate, stay and chat a little longer than you might at other tables.

If you take a personal interest in solo diners they will show more interest in you at the end of the meal. Hint: parties of one can tip <u>extremely</u> well!

18

Have an opinion about your wines

Many guests will look to you for guidance regarding the wines on your list and it is only appropriate that you are able to provide it.

At the least, you should have tasted all (or most of) your wines, know what labels you have available, know how to pronounce each wine properly and be able to describe your wines to your guests (red or white, sweet or dry, full or light-bodied, and so forth.) The more you know, the more help you can be to your guests.

Even better, taste your wines with the different foods you offer. If you form an opinion about which wines you think go best with each of the items on your menu, you will be able to share your views with your guests when it seems appropriate.

19

Reinforce the guests' decisions

Nobody likes to make a mistake, so people can feel particularly vulnerable whenever they have to make a decision. As an extreme example, imagine how you would feel if you ordered something in a restaurant and the waiter rolled his eyes and laughed!

A few encouraging comments from you can reassure your guests that they are making wise choices. The better they feel about their decisions, the more likely they will be to order additional items and try new things.

Even if what they choose is not your favorite, you can still reinforce the decision. You can say "That's one of our most popular items," or "Jack, one of our waiters, just raves about that!" or "I think you're really going to like that!" You get the idea.

20

Make it easy for large groups

Going out to eat with a large group of people can be a hassle. It is particularly awkward when the party first sits down and everyone is trying to get settled in. If the meal gets off to a good start, it is likely to be more fun for you (and for everyone at the table!)

Recommend a selection of appetizers for the group to share. At least a few of the items should be ones that you can deliver quickly. Find out if they want separate checks and if they do, offer to divide the cost of the appetizers equally between the Diners.

If they don't want appetizers, bring bread or something else to nibble on. Get some beverages on the table fast. Make it easier and more pleasant for the group and they will want to take better care of you,

21

Bring extra napkins when appropriate

Speaking from experience, the napkin a man uses to remove the BBQ sauce from his moustache will be too soiled for him to want to place it back in his lap! So a gentleman with a moustache or beard really needs two napkins — one to put in his lap and one to keep his face clean!

Some items are so messy that most <u>everyone</u> will want an extra napkin. This can be particularly true with "finger foods" like overstuffed sandwiches, ribs or fried chicken.

Families dining with young children will need extra napkins to clean up their kids and the mess they inevitably make. Don't make a big fuss, just bring extra napkins early in the meal. It's a good way to show guests you understand their needs.

22

Let guests off the hook

Accidents happen. Guests will knock over a drink, drop their silverware, upset a chair or worse. These incidents are embarrassing for everyone at the table and particularly for the guest who made the error. If the guest's mood drops, your tip can drop along with it.

Keep your perspective and your sense of humor. Correct the situation or remove all evidence of the error quickly and quietly. A simple phrase like "Don't worry, it happens all the time" can take spotlight off the incident, defuse what might otherwise be a disastrous evening and help everyone relax.

Above all, avoid showing any displeasure at the incident. We all make mistakes and nobody likes to have it rubbed in their face. A pleasant evening comes from taking the pressure <u>off</u> rather than putting it on!

23

Take good care of the kids

Going out to eat with children, especially young ones, can be like trying to nail jello to the wall! It is trying at best and a struggle at worst.

Children are your guests, too, but many servers treat kids like non-people — talking to the parents instead of the youngsters and generally ignoring the little guys. No wonder children can go to extremes to get noticed!

Go out of your way to give kids a little extra (personal) attention. Give them their own menu whether or not they might be able to read it. Get them something to play with. Even a blank piece of paper and a pencil is better than nothing. Parents love people who love their kids and if the children are happy, the parents will be thrilled (a situation from which you can profit!)

24

Pass some good news to the cooks

In the same way that you need to be sensitive to the mood of your guests, you will also benefit from being sensitive to the kitchen crew. If you have the support of the kitchen, it will be a lot easier to take exceptionally good care of your guests!

Think about it. The cooks are back there knocking themselves out to produce a great product under some very extreme conditions. If the only time they hear from you is when something is wrong, what do you think happens to their mood and their eagerness to help you? To foster harmony, share some good news with the cooks on your trips to the kitchen. Don't break their concentration, but be sure to let them know when guests are loving the food. Treat the dish crew with respect, too. They can also help you out!

25

Replace soiled serviceware

You wouldn't set the table with dirty silver-ware, would you? The answer is obvious but many servers think nothing of handing a soiled fork back to the diner when they remove the salad bowl, often with a comment like "You'll need this later." How rude! Every time you clear a course, simply remove any silverware the guest has left on the plates you are clearing — even if it looks clean. Then bring a clean replacement automatically — no fuss, no need to ask.

If they comment about it, you could say something like "We would never ask you to eat with soiled silverware." Even if your guests don't notice when you bring clean silver, they are likely to notice when your competitors <u>don't!</u> And when that happens, who do you imagine they will they think of?

26

Refold an absent guest's napkin

When guests leave the table during the meal, they usually place their napkin on the table or on the seat of their chair. As you are passing the empty chair, quietly pick up the napkin and refold it. Place the folded napkin in a spot where the guest will notice it when they return — over the arm of the chair, beside the place setting or on the back of the chair.

This small gesture is so uncommon that (in the right restaurant) it can be quite impressive. Keep your movements casual — it could seem pretentious if you call attention to what you are doing or if you have a smug look on your face when you do it.

(This only works with cloth napkins — it doesn't have the same impact with paper!)

27

Recognize lefties

The standard service setting (position of the water glass, coffee cup, etc.) is set up for right-handed people. Most of the time this is not an issue but it can occasionally present a minor irritation for your left-handed guests.

If you are a lefty, you know what I mean. If you are not, watch how a left-handed diner will often move their water glass, etc. to the left side where it is easier for them to grasp naturally.

When you notice that a guest is left-handed, serve their beverages on the left (or wherever they have placed them). There is no right or wrong here, strictly a matter of making it as easy as possible for the guest. It's a small touch, but it will show your guests that their well-being is important to you.

28

Bring the full one before taking the empty one

This is a very subtle service enhancement but it is worth noting. Let's say a table of diners needs more rolls. At the lowest level of service, the guests will notice that the rolls are low and ask you for more.

You know it is always better if you notice the need before the guests do, but if you take the empty roll basket and return with a full one, for a short period your guests may feel a bit diminished. You took something away from them. It leaves a psychological "hole" on the table where the rolls used to be.

However, if you bring a full basket <u>before</u> taking the empty one away, you are always adding to what the guests have. They are never left without, they will feel better served . . . and they will feel better about you, too!

29

Speak in complete sentences

We have a tendency to use shorthand when talking to guests. ("Smoking or non?" "More rolls?" "Coffee?") While it is understandable, such shortcuts do not help your guests feel exceptionally well cared-for.

Just adding a few words to turn the phrase into a sentence can help create a higher level of service for your guests. ("Do you have a seating preference?" "Can I bring you more rolls?" " Would you like hot coffee?")

Speaking in complete sentences forces you to think before you open your mouth. This helps you drop distracting thoughts and helps create the personal connection that will ultimately determine your tip. Complete sentences don't take any more time . . . and you can pick up points for your extra effort.

30

Give guests something good to talk about

Word-of-mouth may be the best advertising, but there can be no word-of-mouth without something to talk about! If you want guests to tell their friends about your place (and if you want them to come back more often), you have to educate them as to why they come to your restaurant in the first place.

When you sense a natural opening, tell them something they didn't know about the food or the restaurant, pass some inside information or give them a pleasant surprise.

Remember if you want guests to talk about you, it's not enough that they had a good time – in order to talk they need to know <u>why</u> they had a good time. When they have something to talk about, they will have something to tell others!

31

Offer to make copies

Job One is to be sure the guests are happy. One way to have that happen is for you to do something they wouldn't think to ask for. Here's an idea that might work:

If you have a copy machine in the restaurant and you have a table full of business people involved in a meeting, you might ask if they would like you to make copies of any notes or documents. If you have a FAX machine, you could offer that as a service, too.

The offer can't hurt and will show your desire to help them accomplish what they came to do. To be safe, it might be wise to have your manager's approval of this idea before you start to offer these services to guests but it is a very simple gesture with little cost that can bring you and the restaurant big rewards.

32

Be an advocate for your guests

Good service is simply finding out what people want, learning how they want it and helping them get it just that way.

Most of the time things work pretty smoothly but occasionally guests may have a request that seems to be at odds with a house policy. If that happens, don't argue with the guest or tell them what you <u>can't</u> do. See if you can find a way to work around the rules and help them get what they need.

In an ideal world there would never be a discrepancy between the needs of the guest and a policy of the business but sometimes it happens. When it does, make a note of irritating policies and look for how they might be changed to work for the guest without compromising the needs of the restaurant.

33

Anticipate guests' needs

If you keep your head clear and stay out of "the weeds," you can usually sense what your diners need before they ask you for it. For example, some menu items are likely to call for a certain condiment. Guests who are sharing a dish will need an extra plate and perhaps an extra piece of silverware. Someone who drops a fork will need a clean one. Someone in a hurry wants you to share their urgency and move quickly.

It helps to be on the lookout for guests who are looking for you. Scan people's faces as well as the tabletop when you return to your station. Every time diners have to ask for something, it shows a missed opportunity to pick up some points. The fewer of these possibilities you miss, the better cared-for your guests will feel. Make it a game to be a mind-reader.

34

Take the picture

If guests arrive with a camera, there is probably a reason for it, most likely a special event they wish to record.

Offer to take a picture of the party so that everyone can be included in the shot. They may ask you to do it anyway, but you won't pick up any bonus points if they bring up the idea first. Be sure to treat their camera with respect and ask questions if you are not sure how to operate it. They will appreciate your concern for their property.

To *really* knock some socks off, have your own Polaroid and offer to take a free picture of festive groups of diners! It would be a great idea if management provided one for just this purpose but even if they don't, it is your income at stake. Helping others have fun is one of the most rewarding parts of this work.

35

Move with the speed of the room

Good service is invisible. That is, it never detracts guests from the reason they came out — to be with their friends and enjoy a pleasant meal. A frantic server charging around in an otherwise calm dining room can be a major distraction for guests. When it happens, it may diminish both their experience of the meal and your tip.

To avoid this lapse of service, try being invisible by moving at the speed of the room. If the pace of the meal service is lively, move more quickly. If the feeling in the room is relaxed, your movements should be slower.

If you move at the speed of the room, your activities will never be a distraction and your guests will have a better time. It takes some practice but it can be fun!

36

Bring wetnaps for small children

Children get into everything so you know that parents will need to clean up kids' sticky fingers before the meal and again after they eat. In anticipation of this need, why not bring wetnaps or a moist towel before the parents have to ask or before they start to use their own supply? You will show your understanding and help to make the dining experience more pleasant.

It's a tough job to dine out with kids so do what you can to help. Bring a few packets of crackers for the little ones to toss around. That's what they *do* with them, of course, but it is better to have to clean up a few crumbs than to have to clean up the mess made to every other guest's dining experience by a wailing baby or a rampaging toddler. It is a nice thing to do for the parents, too!

37

Resolve problems immediately

A service pro will notice (and correct) minor annoyances before they have a chance to grow into complaints. If you sense that a guest is not delighted, make it right — right now. No excuses, no hassles.

There is no way to effectively resolve a complaint other than in favor of the guest and the sooner, the better. If you have an upset guest, you must address the upset and not the circumstances behind it. <u>Why</u> they are upset is not important. It may not even have anything to do with the restaurant or with you, but make it right anyway. The cost of keeping a guest is always less than the cost of losing one. If guests don't have a good memory of their visit, they won't come back and that will be a huge blow to everyone's income!

38

Place the coffee cup handle at 4:00

This should be an automatic part of any coffee or tea service, but it seems to be so uncommon these days that you can actually pick up points for doing it. Simply to place the cup on the appropriate spot on the table and then <u>rotate</u> the cup until the handle is in the proper position for the guest to grasp it. This is usually on the right side with the handle at 4:00 for right-handers and on the left side with the handle at 8:00 for left-handed guests.

If the cup is served on a saucer, rotate the saucer to place the handle in position. If you use a mug, be careful to keep your fingers well away from the lip of the mug when you turn it. This is a small touch that will help your guests see how much you care for them . . . and it can't hurt to do that!

39

Ask permission before refilling coffee

If you drink coffee any way but black, you know that coffee drinkers have a certain balance of coffee, cream and sugar that they really like.

If you top off the cup without permission, you upset that balance and risk irritating the guest. Just ask permission before you refill the cup and you will stand out from most of your competitors. The same holds true for iced tea or any other beverage that the diner may have "doctored up" to taste.

Be sure, too, that guests always know when you have refilled a cup with hot coffee. People can space out anything and you don't want an accidental scalding because a diner didn't notice that you added hot coffee to a cup they expected to be cooler!

40

Say "decaf" quietly when pouring it

People who drink decaf are always being offered refills of "high test" by servers who don't know (or care) what was supposed to be in the cup. It is an on-going irritation that decaf drinkers can easily live without.

Quietly saying "decaf" when pouring it is a subtle way to reassure guests that they are getting the proper brew. This will reduce their anxiety every time the cup is refilled and a relaxed guest is a happier guest. This can be a special touch at banquets when coffee pots may not be as clearly marked.

It helps to have a positive way to identify what type of coffee the guest is drinking. A colored coaster is one way to identify cups of decaf. One restaurant even uses different colored mugs! No mistakes there!

41

Bring a fresh cup of coffee

Sometimes the guest orders coffee and the half-full cup just sits on the table. Once the coffee is cold, the best that topping it off will do is to bring the temperature up to somewhere around lukewarm!

If a partially-full cup has been sitting for a while, either bring the diner a full cup of hot coffee or bring a clean cup and fill it at the table. This may present a chance for you to educate the guest as to what you are doing for them (remember what we said about word-of-mouth) and help them be aware of the extra service you are providing.

This simple gesture will assure the guest will have a hot, satisfying cup of coffee and you will have shown how much you care. Both will work to your benefit when it comes time for them to figure the tip!

42

Offer complimentary coffee refills on espresso

You would refill the cup if guests had ordered a cup of coffee, so why not make the same offer to those guests who order espresso, cappuccino, or other specialty coffee drinks?

Suggest a second cup of espresso (or whatever) first, of course, but if they decline, offer a refill of regular coffee. This pleasant surprise will make for happier guests and help you stand out from other restaurants that are not as service-oriented.

Coffee time is important because you want to be sure your guests leave with a positive last impression of their meal. This is also the time when they are deciding what sort of tip they will leave. After running a good race, don't blow it by losing your concentration and falling down at the finish line!

43

Settle the check quickly

When the guests have indicated that they are ready to settle up, take care of it promptly. Deliver the check at once and process the payment quickly as well. They may be in a hurry, particularly if you have given them a relaxing experience. At the very least, they have indicated they are ready to go and it is disrespectful if you do not to honor their wishes.

If they pay by cash, make sure the change is correct. Bring enough small bills for a tip but don't be too blatant about it. Never assume a tip and keep the change. If they pay by credit card, include a pen (and be sure it works!) This is when guests actually leave you the tip so your service at the end must be as cordial as your service at the beginning. Continue to give the party your attention until they are out the front door.

44

Garnish the doggie bag

If you pack your guests' leftovers to take home, give it the same care and attention you give everything you do for them.

Be proud of your food and treat it with respect. Unless your local health department prohibits it, always pack up leftovers in the kitchen, never at the table. It is difficult to load a take home container in an appetizing manner at the table.

Arrange the food attractively and then add something the guests didn't expect. It could be a garnish, extra sauce on the pasta or a container of tortilla chips with the Mexican leftovers. You will knock your guests' socks off when they get home! This little surprise can help endear you to your diners and is an investment in their future patronage. It is also great fun!

45

Help with the coats

This is another bit of common courtesy that has largely fallen into disuse and for that reason it can gain you good will at the end of the meal.

A general rule is to hold coats for the ladies, starting with the elders. Hand coats to the men or assist them as seems appropriate. If there are children in the party, hand their coats to the parents and assist adults after the kids are dressed.

While this gesture won't affect your tip today, it might leave guests with a better memory of their experience and make them inclined to return a little sooner. At the least, a repeat visit will increase sales for the restaurant and put more money in the tip pool. At best, the guests will ask for you next time and become your regular patrons.

46

Invite guests back on a specific day for a specific reason

The safest way to build sales is by getting guests to return more often. "Y'all come back" is pleasant, but it isn't likely to move people to action. You will generate more repeat business with something specific.

If it seems appropriate, you might make a comment like, "Come back next Thursday for our fajita special. It's really a great deal. I'll be working that night and I would really enjoy seeing you again." This is more apt to create a return visit than a simple "thank you."

Inviting guests to ask for you when they return will help you build a regular following. You may have a few loyal patrons already. Today's strangers can become tomorrow's regulars . . . and regulars usually tip better!

47

Check for forgotten articles immediately

Children, especially the little ones, are always dropping things. Dining out with kids is tough enough without having to come all the way back to the restaurant again to pick up junior's favorite toy.

In the confusion of settling the check, getting the whole crew moving, putting coats on everyone and so forth, it is easy to miss things. It only takes a second to check under the table and in the corners as soon as the family gets up to leave.

Parents will remember (and appreciate) that you found "Boo Bear" hiding under the table before their youngster threw a tantrum about it. Happy guests are more likely to speak well of you, leave a larger tip and return more often!

48

Show your gratitude

Gratitude is powerful and no one gets all the appreciation they deserve. (Do you?) Your guests have many options when it comes to dining out and they will tend to go where they feel their business is truly appreciated. Showing gratitude means more than saying "thank you." In communication, the real message is always carried in the <u>feeling</u> behind the tone of voice that you use, it is not just about your words.

Stay in touch with the feeling of gratitude and it will come through in everything you say. If you have a picture that makes you feel good, keep it in the service stand or in your order pad. It doesn't matter if it is a picture of your kids or your car as long as it helps you stay in touch with good feelings. Gratitude is a powerful way to help assure your guests' good will and future support.

49

Call immediately on lost and found articles

If a guest forgets something and you find it, treat it with respect, protect it . . . and get busy! Try to find out who the person was and where they live. You might have their name from a credit card receipt or someone else on staff might know them.

If you found a credit card, call the issuer's lost card number and notify them that you have the card (in case the guest calls to report a loss). If you know where the guest is, call to say you have their property safely in hand so they will not worry.

Offer to return the item to them yourself, put it in a cab or mail it. If they must come back for it, give them a coupon for a free goodie on their next visit to help make up for the inconvenience. It will pay off for you.

50

Send a thank-you note

To make a real impression on a guest, send a thank-you note the day after they dine with you! This doesn't need to be anything more than a simple "Thank you for coming in and I hope to see you again soon" note.

You may have the diner's name from the credit card. If you have a phone number from the reservation list you can find their address in a reverse telephone directory. There are many ways to get a guest's name if you really want it.

Use this idea with care, particularly with couples — you don't want to unintentionally embarrass anyone! Still, a personal note can be a very effective gesture . . . provided you connected with the guests during the meal and provided the sentiment truly comes from your heart!

REMEMBER:

Guests only leave good tips because they *want* to!

Getting the most from this book

This little book can help you do a better job, have more fun and make more money. Now you can certainly use it any way you like but sometimes it helps to have a strategy when you start to work with new ideas. Here are some suggestions on how to get the most from this material.

There are three important things to remember about making changes:

- Don't take on too many new ideas at once. You might get overwhelmed and go back to your old habits.

- Keep track of what is working. It is fun to notice improvement and it will make it easier to continue.

- Be patient. These tips are all subtle enhancements to service and none of them are likely to double your bank account in a week. In the tip improvement game, as in weight loss, slow, steady progress is more likely to produce lasting results.

You don't have to be bad to get better, so here's how you can use this book to improve:

As a start, read through the book a few times. You will probably find that several of the suggestions are already part of your regular service routine — a validation that you are already on the right track.

1. Establish a baseline (hours worked, tip income, tip percentage) based on the last few weeks. NOTE: this is strictly for your own information unless you choose to share it.

2. Pick one of the 50 tips each week and work only on that one notion for the week. It might help if every server selects a different item each week but it is not necessary.

3. Review the selected item frequently. Read the "page of the week" before each shift and on breaks. It may help to write the tip down a few times.

4. Try to work the item into the service on every table but be sensitive to your guests — don't force it if it doesn't seem appropriate. If you forget, remind yourself and pick it up again at the next table. Remember that you have to do something 21 times to make it a habit.

5. Focus only on the tip of the week. Resist the urge to introduce anything else new into your service during the week. You have plenty of time.

6. Keep track of observable results each day (hours worked, tip income, tip percentage, guests who ask for your station and diner comments.)

7. Compare your weekly results to the baseline and to what you did last week. Notice any improvements.

8. Work together. Talk with any co-workers who may have already worked on the tip you select each week. Share ideas based on your experience of working with each of the ideas.

9. Once you are comfortably using the new idea, pick another one to work on and continue this process. Continue to use the tips you have worked on in prior weeks. You will steadily improve your level of guest service . . . and your income!

So that's the plan if you want to get serious about it. If you prefer to be more casual in using these notions, it is your income and your choice.

Whatever you do, have fun and remember that Job One is to make sure the guests are happy!